Hawai Guide on a Budget

A Guidebook for Affordable Travel in the Most Beautiful State

By

Jeffrey Gray

© **Copyright 2020 - All rights reserved.**

The content contained within this book may not be reproduced, duplicated or transmitted without direct written permission from the author or the publisher.

Under no circumstances will any blame or legal responsibility be held against the publisher, or author, for any damages, reparation, or monetary loss due to the information contained within this book, either directly or indirectly.

Legal Notice:

This book is copyright protected. It is only for personal use. You cannot amend, distribute, sell, use, quote or paraphrase any part, or the content within this book, without the consent of the author or publisher.

Disclaimer Notice:

Please note the information contained within this document is for educational and entertainment purposes only. All effort has been executed to present accurate, up to date, reliable, complete information. No warranties of any kind are declared or implied. Readers acknowledge that the author is not engaged in the rendering of legal, financial, medical or professional advice. The content within this book has been derived from various sources. Please consult a licensed professional before attempting any techniques outlined in this book.

By reading this document, the reader agrees that under no circumstances is the author responsible for any losses, direct or indirect, that are incurred as a result of the use of the information contained within this document, including, but not limited to, errors, omissions, or inaccuracies.

Table of Contents

The Best Time of Year to Visit the Hawaiian Islands: 4

    The Hawaiian Islands in the Winter: 4

    The Hawaiian Islands in the Spring: 6

    The Hawaiian Islands in the Summer: 7

    The Hawaiian Islands in the Fall: 8

How to Get to the Hawaiian Islands on a Budget: 10

Traveling Around and Between Islands on a Budget: ... 15

    Traveling Around the Hawaiian Islands – 15

    Traveling Between the Hawaiian Islands - 18

Where to Stay in the Hawaiian Islands on a Budget 21

Free and Cheap Things to do on Each Island 37

How to Eat on a Budget 55

    Where to Eat on a Budget – Big Island: 57

    Where to Eat on a Budget – Oahu: 58

    Where to Eat on a Budget – Maui: 59

    Where to Eat on a Budget – Lanai: 60

    Where to Eat on a Budget – Molokai: 61

    Where to Eat on a Budget – Kauai: 63

Best Money-Saving Websites to Book your Trip 65

How to Keep Safe 69

   Here are the Visitor Assistance numbers for the main Hawaiian Islands: 72

Top-Tips and Hacks to Save Money 73

Hawaii – the breathtaking and completely magical tropical paradise that has captivated the hearts of adventurers and island-lovers for centuries. It offers its visitors a whole host of varying geographical landscapes, from the multitude of active volcanoes, some of the world's tallest mountains, such as Mauna Kea, which is inherently sacred to Hawaiians, as well as the sheer abundance of soft sandy beaches and crystal clear blue waters. In addition to these picture-postcard-level examples of Hawaii's natural gems, the islands also offer a slow-paced and relaxing way of life that welcomes its visitors with open arms. After you visit the wonders of Hawaii you will inevitably feel as though you have left a piece of your heart there.

Many people refer to Hawaii very broadly, though many people don't realize that Hawaii is just one of many islands that make up a larger archipelago in the North Pacific Ocean. There are six main islands in The Hawaiian Islands: Kauai, Oahu, Molokai, Lanai, Maui, and finally, the largest of all, Hawaii. Though Hawaii is a state of the United States of America, it very much has its own national identity and traditions and it feels an entire world away from the USA; the islands are one of the most geographically isolated spots on the planet, and there is an eye-wateringly staggering distance of 2,400 miles to the nearest mass of land, which is California. The islands were formed approximately 75 million years ago as a result of volcanic activity. Though there are many islands in existence, there are still new ones forming deep beneath the surface of the sea. The islands are a geographical masterpiece and continue to inspire a multitude of visitors, from scientists and geologists, to honeymooners, foodies and families.

When you picture Hawaii, however, your mind most likely jumps to images of luxury resorts, expensive coastal Michelin Star restaurants and lavish island tours that are far from the means of budget traveling. Yet, scratch beyond the surface of these expectations and you will discover, with the help of this in-depth breakdown, that budget travel to The Hawaiian Islands is indeed a possibility. Though there are far cheaper places to travel to in the world, in terms of transportation, accommodation and activities, there is nowhere that beats the feeling of coming in to land and witnessing first-hand the splendor and glory of the dots of land from a birds-eye view, and the sheer excitement of what lies ahead.

There is a multitude of ways to save money when visiting The Hawaiian Islands, from thinking creatively about where and how you eat, to searching for discounted activities and local events, as well as thinking outside the box when deciding where to stay. It is also arguable that by budget traveling to Hawaii you will have a more authentic, enjoyable, and memorable experience by engaging with the locals and seeing the side of the islands that are frequently bypassed by resort-goers and package holidays. This guide will inform you on the best ways to save money in a whole host of ways, without compromising on the quality of your trip.

The Best Time of Year to Visit the Hawaiian Islands:

There is no correct or best time to visit Hawaii since it remains completely beautiful throughout the year, there are, however, pros and cons of traveling in a particular season. From flight prices, availability, accommodation costs, weather and how crowded the islands are, each season can alter your overall experience -- and by being more flexible with the time of year in which you travel, you can potentially save yourself a huge amount of money. This section of the guide will provide an informative and in-depth explanation of the benefits of each season, when traveling on a shoestring budget.

The Hawaiian Islands in the Winter:

From the middle of December onwards, Hawaii is often very busy, and in the more populated areas of the islands, you will find many more crowds than usual. A key reason for this is that during the winter many visitors flock to the island for whale watching. At this time, the Humpback Whales migrate from Alaska and can be spotted birthing their young. Regarding the weather, whilst many states in the USA are attempting to keep warm throughout the winter, the Hawaiian Islands are still incredibly warm and sunny, with an average daily temperature standing at around 78 degrees.

If you like to partake in a lot of events while traveling, winter is also a great time to visit the islands; there are many holiday traditions and activities taking place that are open to both visitors and locals alike. For example, there is a yearly parade of Christmas lights where places like Honolulu are lit up brightly, and there are a lot of festivities taking place, such as parties, concerts, and other performances, as well as just a generally friendly and welcoming atmosphere.

If you are most attracted to the natural scenery and outdoor activities of the Hawaii Islands, the winter is a great time to visit, as the temperatures are comfortably warm and sunny, and it is the idyllic climate for hiking. If you are a keen swimmer, however, this time of year is not the best for oceanic activity as the currents and rougher and more dangerous.

Overall, the winter, or as it is locally known as, "Ka Hoolio," is a good time to visit for the temperature, festivities and general atmosphere, though because it is a peak season, it will be more crowded and expensive.

The Hawaiian Islands in the Spring:

If you are a sun-worshipper, there is arguably no better time to visit the Hawaiian Islands than the spring, or as the locals refer to it, "Waipuna." At this point in the year, the weather becomes much drier and the sun is out in its full glory. It is also the point in the year where the island comes to life in color, as the beautiful flowers start to re-bloom after the winter; it is truly a magical time of year.

There are also a lot of outdoor activities and festivals that begin in spring; some of which include the Merrie Monarch Festival, which takes place every year on the Big Island of Hawaii and commences every Easter Sunday. There is also the May Day Lei Day, which is an enormous celebration of all things happy, such as singing, dancing, and flowers. There is also a vast number of Hula Festivals, which celebrate many of the islands' historic traditions and is a wonderful experience as a visitor.

The spring is also a fantastic time to visit Hawaii if you love the beach; the waters are far calmer and more predictable than they are in the winter, which means that they are in the perfect condition for swimming. Due to this calmness, however, surfing activities generally tend to dry up, as the waves are simply not big enough.

Overall, spring is fantastic time to visit the Hawaiian Islands. Flight prices and accommodation also typically drop during this period and the crowds are not as intense as they are at other points in the year. Spring is arguably the best time to visit the islands for the budget traveler.

The Hawaiian Islands in the Summer:

Though the Hawaiian Islands are simply breathtaking at this time of year, due to the bright and delicious sunshine, it is most definitely the busiest season. It is this time of year that many of the schoolchildren are on summer vacation, meaning there are a lot of families visiting, particularly in the month of July. If you are travelling as a family, it is still nonetheless a great time of year to visit but it is important to note that it may be a little crowded in certain areas. If you are more flexible throughout the year, it may be more advisable to visit at a quieter period, such as the spring.

Regardless, there are still a lot of great activities going on throughout the islands during the summer that are suitable for families, couples, or even individual travelers. If you are a bit of a foodie or wine enthusiast, there is the fantastic Kapalua Wine and Food Festival that takes place in the summer to celebrate global grapes and cuisine, as well as many local options as well. If you love to explore the ins and outs of a culture when visiting somewhere new, make sure to check out the Aloha Festivals, which celebrate Hawaiian traditions and history, as well as the Honolulu Made in Hawaii Festival, which focuses on local arts and crafts. Duke's OceanFest is also a fantastic festival that celebrates Hawaiian beach and water activities, which are fundamental to its national identity.

Overall, Hawaii and its islands are absolutely beautiful during the summer, and there are a lot of activities and festivals to enjoy, particularly if you are traveling as a family. The prices, however, do jump up at this time, and it may be harder to find available accommodation on a budget.

The Hawaiian Islands in the Fall:

Like spring, the fall is also a particularly good time to visit the Hawaiian Islands; it promises its visitors warm weather, calm waters perfect for swimming, and fewer crowds, which also means generally cheaper prices for flights and accommodation. There are also often many more discounts on activities and events. If you live in a colder country, the Hawaiian Islands are the perfect place to escape to during the chilly autumnal months.

There are a lot of events going on at this time that cater to a wide variety of visitors, including the amazing Kona Coffee Festival, which celebrates coffee growers and farmers from the islands, as well as other coffee-based snacks, chocolates and cakes. The Hawaii Food and Wine

Festival takes place every fall, which is the perfect festival for anyone who enjoys trying new cuisines and considers themselves a bit of a foodie. It is also a great opportunity to mix with the locals and sample new and unique ingredients, and to purchase souvenirs to take home with you.

Because children have gone back to school and parents have gone back to work, the fall is a quiet time of year, but the weather remains warm and inviting; you will often find that you may have an entire beach to yourself, which is the perfect way to spend a sunny afternoon. It is also at this point in the year that the waves start picking up again, and without the crowds, it is a great time to pick up a surfboard and learn a new skill.

How to Get to the Hawaiian Islands on a Budget:

Because the Hawaiian Islands are so isolated and far away from any landmass, (2,400 miles in total to California), it is inevitably going to be expensive to get to initially; however, there are many ways in which you can instantly shed money off of your flights, just by being a little bit savvy. This part of the guide will provide you with the top tips and hacks on getting to the Hawaiian Islands on a budget:

- Among the Islands, Oahu is the major airport in Hawaii, and is where the majority of travelers will arrive. Once you have arrived you can still travel between the islands, such as Maui, Kauai and the Big Island through Oahu's Daniel K. Inouye International Airport.
- However, there are airlines from North America that travel direct to other Hawaii Island airports, which are as follows:
- From **North America direct to Maui's Kahului Airport** airlines include Alaska Airlines, American Airlines, Air Canada, Delta

Airlines, WestJet, United Airlines, and Hawaiian Airlines.
- From **North America direct to Kailua-Kona on Hawaii's Big Island** airlines include Alaska Airlines, Delta Airlines, Air Canada, American Airlines, Hawaiian Islands, Delta Airlines, United Airlines and WestJet.
- From **North American direct to Lihue, Kauai** airlines include WestJet, United Airlines, Air Canada, Alaska Airlines, Delta Airlines, American Airlines, and Hawaiian Airlines.
- From **North America direct to Hilo on Hawaii's Big Island** airlines include just United Airlines and Hawaiian Airlines.
- There are also many cities in North America from which can fly to Hawaii and its islands, including: Los Angeles, San Francisco, Seattle, Chicago, Portland, New York JFK, Phoenix, Las Vegas, Anchorage, Salt Lake City, Atlanta, Newark, and Vancouver.
- If you are traveling from Asia, however, there are also a number of budget airlines that fly direct to the Hawaiian Islands, including AirAsia, Scoot and Jetstar, many of which offer great prices, especially if you look at the correct times.
- One of the best tips for saving money when traveling to Hawaii, is to go out of the peak

seasons, which are the winter and the summer. This is a great option if you are flexible with times, as you really can save a lot of money this way, and the island is much quieter than usual.
- If you are tied down to school holidays, for example, ensure that you book your trip at least three months in advance; this way, you will definitely save more money.
- Another money-saving hack when booking flights, is to not be particular about flying on a specific day. If you have a little more leeway, you can save huge amounts of money by just shopping around and seeing which dates offer the cheapest prices, availability, and the best flying times.
- Flying economy is another, and perhaps obvious, way of saving money when traveling to Hawaii, as business or first class are often extortionately more expensive.
- Use any air miles that you might have to save money on your trip; also check what your credit cards might offer, as there are often many benefits available.
- Use flight comparison websites, such as Skyscanner, Kayak, and Momondo, all of which browse the cheapest flights available for a particular date or month, and redirect you to the

appropriate website. Rather than booking the first flight that you see and believe is a fair and reasonable price, it is well worth spending some time shopping around before booking, as you may come across some fantastic deals.

- Another great tip for saving money when traveling to the Hawaiian Islands, is to include as many stopovers as you can manage; this is often a long and exhausting way of traveling to the islands, but it can more often than not save you an enormous amount of money. Just ensure that you are flying to comfortable airports that have enough amenities to keep you going for the long layovers. If flying through California, it is advisable to avoid San Francisco where possible, as due to its geographical location and weather conditions, there can often be lots of delays; Los Angeles is a much better option for reliability.
- Another way of saving money when on the flight itself is to bring with you your own snacks and drinks, rather than paying the premium to have food when onboard.
- Flight prices from the mainland USA and the Hawaiian Islands typically range from around $340, particularly if you fly with budget airlines, to $1000.

- If you are flying from Asia to Hawaii, you can expect to pay between $450 and $750.
- If you are flying from Australia to Hawaii, prices typically range from around $500 to $1100.
- Flight prices from Europe to Hawaii are typically the most expensive, ranging from around $850 all the way up to around $1600.

Traveling Around and Between Islands on a Budget:

Unless you envisage your trip to the Hawaiian Islands as a time of sunbathing and purely relaxing in one place for the entirety of your trip, you are more than likely going to want to spend some time hopping between the various islands, and exploring all of the hidden gems that each one has to offer. Although there are numerous islands that make up the archipelago, there are six primary islands that are accessible to tourists: Hawaii Island, or the Big Island; Oahu; Kauai; Molokai; Lanai; and Maui. This section of the guide will explain the various ways that you can travel around the islands, and between them, without breaking the bank.

Traveling Around the Hawaiian Islands –

By Foot: The absolute cheapest way to travel around the Hawaiian Islands is by foot. There are an abundance of famous and iconic hiking trails on each and every island, many of which lead to breathtaking views that veer away from the traditional tourist paths. Some of the best hiking trails on the Big Island include Kilauea Iki, which is situated in the Volcanoes National Park; along this trail, you will experience an array of natural wonders, including the astonishing Crater Rim Trail, lava cracks, rainforest, as well as the local Ohi'a Lehua trees. A great trail to experience on the island of Maui, is to explore the Haleakala National Park; there are gorgeous natural wonders on offer, such as some of the tallest sea mountains in the entire world, and an array of wildlife and coastal views. On the island of Molokai a great place to visit by foot is Kalaupapa, which is a small community of inhabitants; this is a great way to see another side of the island that is not featured on tourist agendas. Hiking and walking are fantastic ways to experience the island, as you can explore hidden gems that are a little off the beaten track.

By Car: Renting a car when visiting the Hawaiian Islands is one of the most common and popular methods of travelling, as it offers full flexibility and freedom. On many of the islands are large and easily recognizable rental companies, including Avis, Dollar, Enterprise, Alamo, National, Thrifty, and Hertz, many of which are located at the airports. Renting a car in the Hawaiian Islands is generally quite affordable, and there are also ways in which you can ensure that you save even more money. Firstly, depending on your needs, rent the smallest and least flashy car that you can get your hands on; this will ensure that you are paying purely for the car and its services, rather than any unnecessary frills. Use websites like Hotwire.com and Priceline.com to find the best deals on car rentals, and also make sure you book far enough in advance to save money. Another money-saving hack when renting a car in Hawaii is to bring you own GPS navigation system; car rental companies can charge a premium for these, and it is definitely an unnecessary cost. Again, if you are flexible with the dates in which you travel to Hawaii, ensure that you go outside of the peak season, as like everything, car rental prices also skyrocket during the tourist season.

By Public Transport: Although traveling around the islands by public transport is one of the cheapest options for exploring, it is by no means the most flexible; though there are bus services, they often do not travel to all of the nooks and crannies and hidden gems that are on offer. On the Big Island, or Hawaii Island, there is a great public bus service, called the Hele-on bus; this is predominately used by local workers, but some budget-travelers also make the most of its services. It is very cheap, though there are long stopover times, and it is not overly reliable; many of the buses also only depart early in the morning or late in the day. In Oahu, there is a public transport service called "TheBus," which offers reasonable and affordable prices, as well as a large selection of routes that can take visitors all over the island. Each of the other key locations, such as Maui and Kauai, has their own public transport services. Maui Bus and Kauai Bus are cheap and affordable, but are sometimes limited. Overall, public transport is a good way to travel Hawaii, but there are limitations.

By Taxi, Lyft or Uber: Another option to use when traveling around the islands is services like Uber and Lyft, or a traditional taxi. Uber and Lyft have been available on the Big Island since 2013, and they are a reasonably affordable way to travel, especially if you are traveling with multiple people, as the price is split and can sometimes work out even cheaper than the bus services. When you visit more remote parts of the islands, you will struggle to find taxis and similar services, but when you are visiting the larger towns and cities, they are a good option.

Traveling Between the Hawaiian Islands -

By Plane: The primary way to travel between the Hawaiian Islands is by plane; on each of the primary six tourist islands, there are airports that offer scenic flights between each of the islands. When flying, you will either fly with Mokulele or Hawaiian Airlines, both of which are local commuter airlines; the shortest flight takes just twenty minutes, whereas the longest flight is fifty minutes, and offers some of the most breathtaking views. These flights are not often overly cheap; however, if you can save money in other parts of your travel in order to be able to spend money on these inter-island flights, it is highly recommendable. The flights themselves are totally unique and thrilling experiences; because the islands are very small, the planes are small as well, and some of them only carry a total of nine passengers! Here is a list of the airports that are gateways to the main six islands:

Big Island, Or Hawaii Island – Ellison Onizuka Kona International Airport at Keahole (KOA) and Hilo international Airport (ITO)

Oahu – Daniel K. Inouye (Honolulu) International Airport (HNL)

Maui – Kahului Airport (OGG) and Kapalua-West Maui Airport (JHM)

Kauai – Lihue Airport (LIH)

Lanai – Lanai Airport (LNY)

Molokai – Molokai Airport (MKK)

By Boat: An alternative to traveling by plane, is to travel between the islands by boat. This service is incredibly limited, however, as the only islands that visitors can actually travel between by boat is Maui and Lanai, which takes approximately fifty minutes. Although this is a good option between these two specific islands, and the prices can be fairly reasonable, it is not possible to travel this way throughout your trip. Alternatively, another way to travel between the islands is on a cruise; many companies offer Hawaiian cruises, such as Princess, Norwegian Cruise Lines and Royal Caribbean. This tends to be a very expensive option, however, and offers less flexibility than many of the other transport options.

Where to Stay in the Hawaiian Islands on a Budget

Finding cheap accommodations on the Hawaiian Islands is not the easiest task; there are a plethora of luxury hotels and apartments with all the frills, but there is a shortage of budget hotels and hostels. Here you will find the best accommodation options available on each of the main islands, as well as the best areas to stay in, without breaking the bank:

Where to Stay on the Big Island on a Budget – Well known for being the largest of the Hawaiian Islands, the Big Island, or otherwise just known as Hawaii Island, is one of the most popular islands to stay in for first-time visitors to the islands. Because it is so large, however, many tourists are unsure as to which area is best to stay in. This list will give you the lowdown on the benefits of each part of the Big Island, and the best places to stay on a shoestring budget:

Best Budget Accommodation in Hilo – Hilo is a fantastic place to stay on the Big Island; it is located on the east side, and has lots of volcanoes nearby. If you are a nature lover and enjoy hiking across the wonderful geographical landscape of Hawaii, Hilo is the ideal place for you. Here are the most affordable places to stay in Hilo that don't break the bank, and also don't compromise on quality:

- Wild Ginger Inn Hotel and Hostel – this is a great place to stay in Hilo, as it is right by the beach, and has a fantastic location that is central to lots of amenities. Prices start from around $400 for two people for 7 days, although this does depend on the time of year that you visit.
- Hilo Bay Hostel – If you are someone who prefers the atmosphere of a hostel when traveling, Hilo Bay Hostel is a great option; there is a really friendly and welcoming vibe, and although it is still not cheap, it is a reasonable price for the area.
- Hilo Reeds Bay Hotel – For a little bit more of a premium, Hilo Reeds Bay Hotel is a great option; for approximately $120 a night, this hotel offers scenic views, comfortable rooms and an array of amazing things to do just on your doorstep.
- The Inn at Kulaniapia Falls – For a truly unique and unforgettable experience, ensure that you stay at The Inn at Kulaniapia Falls, which is an enormous waterfall. The accommodation is located right next to it, and offers some

unbeatable views; it is also a guest house, meaning you have great flexibility and space. Prices start at around $100 dollars a night during the off-peak season.

Best Budget Accommodation in Kailua-Kona – Located on the west side of the Big Island, and offering an abundance of beaches, mountain landscapes and historic hotspots, Kailua-Kona is an incredible place to stay on the island. Kailua-Kona also tends to be a little bit cheaper than Hilo, and it has a much more slow-paced way of life, which is ideal if you are looking to relax. Here are the best places to stay in the area on a budget:

- Simple Kona Guest House – This stunning guest house offers an amazing, unbeatable location in Kaulua-Kona, and also offers rooms with ocean views, which is the perfect thing to wake up to. Prices start from around $90 a night for two people, though this can fluctuate with the season.
- Kona Magic Honu Room – If you prefer your own space when traveling, rather than being cramped up in a small and expensive hotel room, a great place to stay in Kailua-Kona is Kona Magic Honu Room, which is a private accommodation, giving you flexibility and independence, as well as a more authentic experience.

- Kona Islander – Kona Islander is an Aparthotel that is situated right on the beach; it offers light, bright and airy rooms that have lots of space, and also have great views of the surrounding scenery.
- Mango Sunset BnB Inn at Lyman Organic Kona Coffee Farms – For a really fun and welcoming experience that makes you feel right at home, make sure you stay at Mango Sunset BnB Inn; here, you can experience great views and hospitality, as well as lovely coffee, and a quick drive into the hustle and bustle of the city.

Where to Stay on Oahu on a Budget – Out of all of the Hawaiian Islands, Oahu is the most frequently visited, with almost five million visitors every single year. Oahu offers various paces of life and activities depending on where you visit on the island; you can stay anywhere from luxury, high-end resorts that cost a fortune, all the way to budget hotels and hostels. There are four key areas to stay in on Oahu Island, South Oahu, North Shore, the East and Leeward Waianae; this section will provide you with a breakdown of the benefits of each, and some of the best places to stay on a budget:

Best Budget Accommodation in South Oahu – South Oahu is home to some of the most recognizable cities and towns across all the islands, including

Honolulu, Waikiki, and also Kahala. There are a huge variety of hostels and accommodation, as well as a lot of shopping and nightlife options, as well as some of the most beautiful beaches on the entire island. Here are the best places to stay in South Oahu on a budget:

- Polynesian Hostel Beach Club – Feel at one with nature with this coastal hostel in the heart of the vibrant Waikiki. It has a really friendly and welcoming atmosphere, and the prices are very affordable for the area, starting at around $50 a night for two people.
- Kuhio Banyan Hotel – Kuhio Banyan Hotel is a fantastic place to stay in Waikiki; it is affordable, and has a lot of space and amenities, and is within walking distance of lots of bars, shops and restaurants.
- Hostelling International Honolulu – Situated in Manoa in Honolulu, is the Hostelling International Honolulu hostel, which is a perfect option for accommodation; it is very affordable, and has a great international atmosphere where you will meet travelers from around the world.
- Island Colony Studio 2204 – This private apartment is the perfect option for your stay if you prefer a little bit of privacy and space, without breaking the bank; though a little more

expensive than the previous options, this studio is centrally located and has a beautiful terrace.

Best Budget Accommodation in North Shore – If you prefer a slower-paced way of life and fewer crowds, North Shore is the best place to stay on the island; there are so many historical and cultural hotspots to explore, as well as an abundance of natural landscapes and impressive beaches. There is not a huge amount of accommodation options available, however, and they can be a little pricier; here is the best:

- Turtle Bay Resort – Situated on Oahu's scenic North Shore is the fantastic Turtle Bay Resort. This accommodation is definitely not the cheapest, but if you are planning on staying in this area of the island, it is most likely your only option. It offers a luxury feel, impressive views and location, as well as a great restaurant that serves amazing food.

Best Budget Accommodation in East Oahu – If you prefer to stay somewhere a little more off the traditional tourist path and somewhere a little more local and residential, make sure that you stay in Windward East Oahu. Here, you can experience an array of home rentals to get a really authentic experience; there are also lots of natural hotspots and beaches to explore. Because it is less touristy, however, there are fewer eating and entertainment options available. Here is the best budget place to stay in Windward East Oahu:

- Paradise Bay Resort – Very much like the Northern side of the island of Oahu, the East is also very non-touristy, so there are very few options, especially for the budget-conscious traveler. If you do wish to stay in East Oahu, however, the best place you can stay in is the Paradise Bay Resort; it is a short distance from Honolulu Airport, is on the doorstep of many scenic spots and landmarks, and has an abundance of amenities.

Best Budget Accommodation in Leeward Waianae – If you prefer somewhere a little bit more remote and peaceful, Leeward Waianae is a fantastic place to stay; there are lots of accommodation options available and a multitude of quiet beaches, as well as untouched landscapes. This part of the island, however, is the most exclusive, and there are many well-known hotel brands here and luxury resorts. Here is a breakdown of the cheapest places to stay in Leeward Waianae, in the two main spots, Ko Olina and Makaha;

- Marriott's Ko Olina Beach Club – Though definitely not a budget option, the Marriott's Ko Olina Beach Club is one of the slightly cheaper options in the beautiful Ko'Olina region of

Leeward Waianae. It offers guests absolutely stunning rooms with unbeatable views, as well as a true feeling of luxury,

- Four Seasons Resort Oahu at Ko Olina – The Four Seasons hotel chain is known for exuding real luxury, and the resort at Ko Olina is no exception; this is the perfect place to stay if you are traveling for a special occasion.
- Owen's Retreat – If you prefer to have your own independent space when traveling, and feel as though you have your own home away from home, Owen's Retreat is the perfect accommodation. For what you get, this is an incredibly reasonably priced accommodation; it is right on the beach, and has three spacious bedrooms.

Where to Stay on Maui on a Budget – The beautiful island of Maui is one of the most popular and common places to stay within the Hawaiian Islands, and there is huge range of activities to do, and natural treasures to explore. There are a plethora of wonderful beaches, coastal resorts and mountainous landscapes; there are also a lot of types of accommodation, some that cater to high-end budgets, and others that are more aligned to the needs of the budget traveler. This list will provide you with an insight into the top four areas of the island to stay in, the benefits of each, and some budget accommodation options for each:

Best Budget Accommodation in West Maui – If you are unsure where to start when visiting Maui, the west side of the island is ideal; it consistently has fantastic weather, and there are some of the best beaches throughout the entirety of the Hawaiian Islands. The only downside to some is that it can be a little bit touristy, particularly during the peak season, and can get a slightly crowded. Here are some of the best budget-friendly places to stay in West Maui:

- Tiki Beach Hostel – Situated idyllically on the beach in the historic side of West Maui is the Tiki Beach Hostel, which is a great option for budget travelers; it is centrally located and has many amenities right on its doorstep.
- The Lahaina Beach House – Another great option is the Lahaina Beach House, which is a centrally located hostel that offers the traditional dormitory style setup. For the area, this is a great budget option, and is great for solo travelers to meet new people.
- Paki Maui 416 – This fantastic one-bedroom apartment is a great option when staying in the west side of the island; located in the town of Kahana, the apartment is just a short walk to the

beach, and is reasonably priced depending on season in which you visit.

Best Budget Accommodation in South Maui – The south of the island of Maui offers some great benefits, such as its fantastic weather, stunning beaches and hiking trails, as well as a lot of budget accommodation options. There is also more of a local feel in certain parts of it, without the larger stores that are found in other parts of the island. Some of the best places to stay include Wailea and Kihei, and this list will provide some of the best accommodation options within them:

- Hale Huanani B&B – This private residence feels like a home away from home due to its spacious interior, perfect location, and incredible hosts; there is a stunning beach nearby, and it is reasonably priced for the area that it is in.
- Kamaole Sands – This beautiful Aparthotel is a fantastic option if you are looking for somewhere that has space and amenities, without breaking the bank. These one-bedroom apartments are located right by the beach, and also have a lovely swimming pool for cooling down in.
- Maui Parkshore 110 – Situated in the gorgeous Wailea, and just a stone's throw away from the beach, is the Maui Parkshore 110 holiday home

complex; this is an affordable option, and has a fantastic swimming pool and views.
- Maui Banyan Q409A – this private apartment is a great way to experience the island in an authentic and flexible way; it is large, clean, and perfectly located.

Best Budget Accommodation in Central Maui – Central Maui, though beautiful in its own right, is not one of the most scenic parts of the island; the weather tends to be a little more rainy than other parts, there are fewer accommodation options, and there are not as many beaches. On the plus side, it is a much quieter, and there are a great variety of shops in this part. Here is a list of the best budget accommodation options in central Maui:

- The Northshore Hostel Maui – This incredibly central hostel, situated in the town of Wailuku in central Maui is a fantastic option for those who are looking for the cheapest prices possible. It has a friendly atmosphere, and it's a great way to meet fellow travelers.
- Central Maui Hostel – Situated right in the heart of Wailuku is the Central Maui Hostel, which is clean, simple, and reasonably priced; it is central to lots of amenities, and has a great atmosphere.
- Wailuku Guesthouse – If you prefer more space than just a hostel bunk bed, make sure you stay

at the Wailuku Guesthouse; here, you can stay in a lovely comfy bed, be right near the center, and cool off in the shared swimming pool.
- Maui Beach Hotel – Situated in the scenic town of Kahului is the gorgeous and unique Maui Beach Hotel, which is a quirky-shaped structure with a fantastic pool, gorgeous rooms, and a central location, all for a very reasonable price.

Best Budget Accommodation on the Hana Highway – The Hana Highway is a much quieter part of the island than the West and South, but it is incredibly scenic; there are a great variety of picturesque beaches, and it is incredibly peaceful. It can be quite rainy here, however, and it is very isolated, which to some is ideal, and others it is not. Here is the best budget accommodation option on the Hana Highway:

- Aina Kupuna – Aina Kupuna is a wonder holiday home that is great for a large family or group of travelers located in the Maui town of Hana. It is spacious, clean, and in a perfect, central location.

Where to Stay on Kauai on a Budget – Kauai is one of the island's lesser-known and frequently visited islands, though it is absolutely gorgeous; it offers beautiful, luscious mountain landscapes, impressive beaches, an incredible culture and friendliness, and a true sense of tranquility. Because it is so beautiful, accommodation can be very expensive here, and there is no real way to travel here cheaply. There are some options that avoid breaking the bank, however, and they are as follows:

- Kauai Beach House Hostel – This exciting hostel offers the traditional hostel dormitory setup, and has a wonderful and authentic feel; it is cheap, central, clean, and has a really friendly atmosphere, making it a great place to meet people.
- Honu'ea International Hostel Kauai – Another great option if you are a budget traveler and a fan of hostels, is the Honu'ea International Hostel, in the heart of the town of Kapaa. It is clean, tidy, and has a real charm about it.
- Islander on the Beach – If you prefer a little more space and independence when traveling, without breaking the bank, a great place to stay is Islander on the Beach. This is a private one-bedroom apartment that is right on the edge of the beach, meaning it has amazing views and a wonderful location.
- Kauai Palms Hotel – If you prefer a hotel over a self-catered apartment or hostel, make sure to check out Kauai Palms Hotel. This hotel is in

central Lihue and offers visitors unbeatable mountain views.

Where to Stay in Molokai on a Budget – Picture swooping green hills and dramatic coast outlines, with gorgeous deep blue waters lapping against the edges, with practically no human interference, loud, ugly roads, or tall buildings and shopping complexes – this is what the beautiful island of Molokai has to offer. A little off the radar of traditional tourist agendas, Molokai is the perfect island to visit, particularly for those who love hiking, a sense of isolation and unspoiled landscapes. Despite its beauty, however, accommodation can be a little more expensive, and there are often fewer options, making is not so ideal for the budget traveler. Here are the best options nonetheless:

- Castle Molokai Shores – this private Aparthotel offers guests the best of both worlds by having a sense of freedom while also being taken care of. It features beautiful rooms with spectacular ocean views, as well as a very reasonable price tag. It is situated in the heart of Kaunakakai, which has a vast number of amenities, as well as its own charm.
- Paniolo Hale I2 – Situated in the heart of Manualoa, this amazing studio apartment offers

visitors astonishing ocean views from its fantastic balcony. It is spacious, with its large living room, two beds, and bathroom, all of which are incredibly clean and tidy.
- Ka Hale Ola – This fantastic private apartment is located in the gorgeous town of Kaunakakai, which is a hotspot for tourists and visitors; this apartment has wonderful ocean views, lots of space, and is incredibly affordable. With prices starting at around $200 a night in the peak tourist season it is ideal for a couple, and it is incredibly romantic.

Where to Stay in Lanai on a Budget – The smallest inhabited island of the many Hawaiian Islands, Lanai is a real mix of nature and modernity, with its gorgeous, unspoiled natural landscapes, and also an array of high-end luxury resorts. It typically offers travelers some great weather, with mostly sunny spells and calm waters, which makes it perfect for relaxing beach days. There are a lot of accommodation options, but many of them are rather on the expensive side of things, so finding somewhere that is comfortable and reasonably priced can be a bit of a challenge. But here is the best budget option for Lanai Island:

- Hotel Lanai – The island of Lanai is incredibly expensive, so the only real option when staying there without breaking the bank, is Hotel Lanai. Situated in Lanai City, this hotel is definitely not cheap, but it is reasonable. It is clean, offers spacious rooms with gorgeous views, as well as a central location that is not far from the beach.

Free and Cheap Things to do on Each Island

Due to its endless stream of natural treasures and impressive sceneries, there is no shortage of free things to do in the Hawaiian Islands that revolve around emerging oneself in the local landscapes. In addition to the plethora of hiking trails, beaches, and parks that are all free to explore, there are also a vast array of other free, and if not free, incredibly cheap, activities to partake in, such as local food festivals, carnivals, eateries and even certain recreational activities. Though you may spend a little more than average on your accommodation and flights when visiting the Hawaiian Islands, you can certainly spend very little when you are actually there. This list will provide a breakdown of the top then things to do on the main tourist islands of Hawaii: Big Island, Oahu, Maui, Lanai, Molokai and Kauai.

Free and Cheap Things to do on the Big Island (Hawaii) – As the name suggests, Hawaii's Big Island is the largest island in the archipelago, which means that it offers plenty of beaches, parks, and activities that are designed specifically for visitors. There is a whopping 266 miles of coastline and more than 100 beaches that are all free to explore, as well as the abundance of national state parks and volcanoes. Here are the top ten free and cheap things to experience on Hawaii's Big Island:

- Tower above the clouds at Mauna Kea – Head up to the beautiful Mauna Kea, where a Visitors' Information Station holds free stargazing opportunities where you can gaze longingly through telescopes at the expansive night sky. It is also a great place to visit in the daytime, where at nearly 10,000 feet you can look downwards at the clouds.
- Explore Akaka Falls State Park – Feel at one with nature and experience the true natural gems of the Big Island by taking a trip to the Akaka Falls State Park. Situated just to the north of Hilo, walk this relatively easy path and take in the views of the beautiful Kahuna and Akaka Falls.
- Take a history trip to Ka Lae – If you appreciate the historic significance of places when traveling, make sure to take a trip to Ka Lae. Situated on the south of the island, Ka Lae is where the Polynesians first arrived on the island, way back in 750 A.D.
- Explore historic Sacrificial Temples – Located in the Kohala Historical Sites State Monument, you can uncover the famous historic sacrificial temple, or heiau, Mo'okini Heiau. This is

completely free to visit, and has a really fascinating history.
- Take in spectacular views at Polulu Valley Lookout – Witness the dramatic scene of angry waves hitting the Kohala coastline and the jagged, rocky cliffs that tower high above the sea level. In addition to the gorgeous views at Polulu Valley Lookout, the site also has a lot of historic significance attached to it.
- Watch the sun set at Hapuna Beach – The beautiful Hapuna beach, which is situated between Puako and Kawaihae, is equally perfect during the day and night. In the day time, there are luscious sandy beaches and gorgeous waters that make it perfect for family. At sunset, this beach is absolutely stunning, and makes for the perfect location for a romantic evening.
- Partake in water sports at Anaeho'omalu Bay – If you are keen on water sports such as scuba diving, kayaking, and surfing or snorkeling, ensure that you head to Anaeho'omalu Bay. With its unique yellow sands and beautiful waters, this is the ideal place visit.
- Experience Molten Lava – At the Kalapana Lava Viewing Area in the Puna District of the Big Island, witness molten lava spewing dramatically out of the volcano. This is truly an exciting and

thrilling experience that is completely free. Conditions can change very quickly, however, so it is not guaranteed that you will see the lava.

- Visit Lapakahi State Historical Park – At the Lapakahi State Historical Park, which lies to the north of Kawaihae. There is a fantastic ancient coastal settlement historically functioned as a fishing village. There are many remnants from the past on display here and you can also occasionally see humpback whales during the peak season.
- Hilo Famers Market – Situated in Hilo, the Hilo Farmers Market is a spectacle that occurs throughout the year, where more than 200 vendors flock to sell their fresh produce. It is popular with locals and visitors alike and is a great place to just stroll through, taking in the atmosphere, and even trying some local delicacies.

Free and Cheap Things to do on Oahu – Oahu, one of the Hawaiian Island's most popular and frequently visited islands, especially with families or couples, there is no end of cheap and free things to do that allow you to experience the true nature of the island and all of its many charms. Here are the top ten free and cheap things to do on Oahu Island:

- Explore the Koko Crate Trail – If you are someone who loves an adventure and exploring things that feel slightly off the beaten track, make sure to check out the Koko Crate Trail. It is a 2-mile hiking trail along abandoned railroad ties that has many beautiful lookout points along the way.
- Take in some history at the Pearl Harbor National Memorial – Situated in downtown Honolulu the Pearl Harbor National Memorial is an entirety free site to visit. It is the resting place of 1,177 sailors who were killed in the Pearl Harbor attack.
- Oahu Island is Manoa Falls. This 100-foot waterfall is situated to the north of Honolulu and feels a world away from the hustle and bustle of the city. It is also where certain scenes of *Jurassic Park* were filmed.
- Walk the Makapu'u Point Lighthouse Trail – If you are a keen walker and an enthusiast for Hawaii's natural beauty, make sure to embark on the Makapu'u Point Lighthouse Trail where you can experience the expansive coastal scenery, as well as an array of seabirds and whales during season.
- Uncover the artwork at Hawaii State Art Museum – Completely free, the Hawaii State Art Museum

focuses on preserving and displaying art from Hawaii, and makes for a great activity to do on a blistering hot day where you just need to escape the sun!

- Spend an afternoon at the Hoomaluhia Botanical Garden – These beautiful botanical gardens are not particularly popular with tourists, and if you visit them, you will more than likely have a very quiet experience, taking in the beautiful local plants and flowers. There is also great surrounding scenery, which adds to the sense of tranquility.
- Visit Laniakea Beach – Situated between Haleiwa and Waimea Bay, lies the fantastic Laniakea Beach, which makes for a great place to spend relaxing, reading a book, or having a picnic. It is also referred to as Turtle Beach, as many sea turtles can be seen here.
- See a free firework show – Every Friday night there is a tradition in Waikiki: a free firework show presented from the Hilton Hawaiian Village. This is a really fun way to spend an evening and to join in with the locals.
- Go snorkeling and see Oahu's marine life – If you are a keen snorkeler, bring your own equipment with you, and adventure into the oceans. One of the best places to snorkel is Hanauma Bay, which

is near Honolulu, and Shark's Cove, which is on the North Shore.
- Visit Honolulu's historic center – In the center of Honolulu there are an array of historic buildings that transport you to another time and place entirely. This is a great way to see the historic side of Honolulu without spending a penny.

Free and Cheap Things to do on Maui – The second-largest island in the Hawaiian archipelago, Maui is often known as "The Valley Isle," with its impressive and world-renowned beaches, fantastic cuisine, and lookout points to view the migrating humpback whales throughout the winter, many visitors hold Maui near and dear to their hearts, after falling in love with it at first glance. There are also many free and cheap things to do on the island, and here are some of the best:

- Embark on the Lahaina Historic Trail – Enjoy this self-guided tour through 62 historic sites in Lahaina, the beautiful Maui town. The trail spans over 55 acres and you will see a whole array of different sites and natural wonders.
- Enjoy a Friday night party! – Every single Friday night in Maui there is a free party that everyone can join in on. Known as the Friday Town Parties they are sponsored by the County of Maui. They

take place in different places depending on the month. There are local food options available and these parties are enjoyed by locals and visitors alike.
- Explore the Kealia Pong National Wildlife Refuge – If you are a nature and wildlife lover, make sure that you check out the Kealia Pond National Wildlife Refuge, it is completely free. Along this 2,200-foot boardwalk find interesting information about the local wildlife that resides in the area.
- Check out a Hula and Polynesian Dance Show – Hosted at the Ka'anapali Beach Hotel every single night apart from Mondays, this impressive hula show is held at sunset. It is completely free and is a great way to experience some local culture.
- Watch the surfers at Ho'okipa Beach Park – If you are excited by the idea of surfing but are too nervous to get some lessons yourself, check out the professional surfers at Ho'okipa Beach Park located on Maui's North Shore. It is completely free, and can provide hours of entertainment.
- Visit some of Maui's free museums – Maui has several free museums that are perfect to visit if you want to temporarily escape the heat, some of the best include: the Printing Museum at

Lahainaluna High School, Lahaina Heritage Museum, Plantation Museum in the Wharf Cinema Center, and Hale Paahao, which is on Prison Street in Lahaina.

- Travel across a lava field – If you love adventure and doing things that are slightly unusual when on vacation, head to La Perouse Bay where you can drive across an enormous lava field that was formed around 200 years ago. This is a unique and thrilling way to experience the island.
- Explore the forestry at Hosmer Grove – If you love feeling consumed by nature, head towards Hosmer Grove. This forest, though small, is incredibly tranquil, and rarely visited by tourists. With a huge range of trees from all over the world, it is situated near to Haleakala National Park.
- Visit the giant Buddha statue – Feel temporarily transported to Japan by heading to the north of Lahaina where you will find an enormous Buddha statue that is the largest outside of Japan. This is entirely free to check out and is something a little different.
- Watch the sun set over a beach – Maui has a fantastic selection of beaches, all of which offer a beautiful setting for watching the sunset, at no cost at all. Some of the best beaches to watch the

sunset include Kaanapali Beach and Wailea Beach.

Free and Cheap Things to do on Lanai – The smallest island in the archipelago of Hawaii, Lanai is also one of the most charming, and is often the preferred spot for those seeking luxury holidays. But there are also an abundance of free and cheap things to do in Lanai that give visitors a true sense of the island's identity without breaking the bank. Here is a list of the ten best free and cheap things to do on the beautiful islands of Lanai:

- Travel along the Munro Trail – This completely free activity is one of the best things to do on the island of Lanai. Embark on the 12.8-mile path that allows visitors to see all six Hawaiian Islands at once; you will see many different things, ranging from forests, ocean and canyons.
- Check out Shipwreck Beach – Also known by the locals as Kaiolohia, Shipwreck Beach is famously difficult to get to, but for those who do manage, you feel a real sense of achievement. There are several WW2 ships on this beach, as well as several other wrecks.
- For cat lovers, visit Lanai Cat Sanctuary – This free activity is great for those who are cat lovers; it also helps out a good cause. You can pet and

play with the many rescued cats that live at Lanai Cat Sanctuary.

- Relax on Polihua Beach – Situated on the northern shore of Lanai lays the stunning Polihua Beach, which is the perfect location to catch some sun rays, read a book, or simply just take a dip in the warm oceans. There are also many sea turtles on this beach, though they are protected, so make sure that you look but do not touch them.
- Learn some history at the Lanai Culture & Heritage Center – If you are someone who adores learning the history and culture of a new place, make sure to check out the Lanai Culture & Heritage Center, which is located in Lanai City. It is completely free and documents the history of the island, from prehistoric times all the way to modern day.
- Explore Hulopoe Bay – Often at the top of many tourists' agendas when visiting Lanai, Hulopoe Bay is one of the most popular spots with sunbathers and snorkelers. This is one of the safest beaches to visit, and there is such as huge variety of wildlife that live here, both in and out of the ocean.
- Discover the barren Garden of the Gods – This completely free activity is a popular thing to do

for travelers to Lanai. This totally barren and desert-like area feels a world away from the luscious beaches and swooping green hills of the rest of the island.

- Visit the Mike Carroll Gallery – In the center of Lanai City, discover the world-famous Mike Carroll Gallery, which houses some gorgeous artworks by the artist Mike Carroll, as well as several other guest artists. There are a number of different artworks and styles, from photography, all the way to jewelry.
- Check out Pine Isle Market, Ltd. – Explore the fantastic Pine Isle Market, Ltd., which is a great market that provides locals with produce, and has been in service since the year 1951. It is a great spot for tourists and locals alike.
- Go on a road trip – One of the best ways to experience Lanai without breaking the bank is to simply drive around freely and allow yourself to get a little lost. That way, you will see and experience things that are a little off the beaten track, and have a truly unforgettable and memorable experience.

Free and Cheap Things to do on Molokai – Molokai is one of the most fantastic and laid back of the Hawaiian Islands, with a truly slow-paced way of life, minimal human intrusion, as well as some of the best beaches and mountain landscapes throughout the archipelago. A trip to Molokai is truly an island escape and it feels like a real tropical paradise. There also an abundance of free and cheap activities to do here. Here are some of the best:

- Explore Kalaupapa – The sleepy peninsula of Kalaupapa has a 100-year-long history of being a leprosy settlement, and there are several fantastic tours that take you around all of the key areas to give you a detailed history of what went on here. There are also many panoramic hotspots that offer astonishing views.
- Mail a coconut – One of the most unusual but nonetheless fun things that you can do in Molokai on the cheap is to send a coconut to anywhere in the world, whether it be your friends back home, a colleague, your family, or even just to your house to await your return! This service is located at the US Post Office just outside of Ho'olehua.
- Visit Papohaku Beach – The beautiful Papohaku beach is one of the most popular and spectacular spots on the whole island. It is an enormous three-mile-long stretch of sand with crystal clear blue waters. It is great to come here at sunset.
- Experience the North Shore Sea Cliffs – There are two ways to view the stunning and dramatic

North Shore Sea Cliffs: firstly, if you are a strong climber, you can hike to them; alternatively, you can splash out a little bit and take a boat tour, which is an amazing way to experience them. You can also see humpback whales here during the winter.

- Relax on Molokai Harbor – One of the main reasons that people come to Hawaii is simply to just relax, so ensure that you spend some time doing this. A great place to relax on Molokai island is in the harbor; it is completely free, and the ideal way to spend a lazy afternoon reading or sunbathing.
- Go to a live music concert – In Hawaii, across all the islands, a popular activity is to listen to live music. In Molokai, there are many live local music concerts at Hotel Molokai, which is right on the oceanfront. This is a great way to experience local culture on the cheap.
- Hike around Halawa Valley – Situated on the east end of the island, Halawa Valley is an enormous valley that many believe to be the oldest settlement in Hawaii. With its swooping green hills and enormous waterfalls, this is the perfect place to hike and explore.
- Molokai Museum and Cultural Center – If you find yourself wanting to take a breather from the

outdoors and the blistering heat, but still want to learn about the local area, take a trip to Molokai Museum and Cultural Center, which is located just off the Kalae Highway.

- Visit Purdy's Macadamia Nut Farm – This five-acre nut farm offers free daily tours where visitors can discover how nuts are grown, harvested and sold, in a really hands-on way. This is a unique and memorable thing to do in Molokai.
- Spend your Saturday at the Molokai Farmers Market – If you consider yourself a foodie, no trip to Molokai would be complete without a trip to the Molokai Farmers Market, which takes place every Saturday from 7:00am on Alamalma Street. It is free to wander around, but you may be tempted by the beautiful delicacies that are on offer there.

Free and Cheap Things to do on Kauai – Out of all of the Hawaiian Islands, Kauai is the oldest. It is also very small, though it has some of the finest beaches, rainforests, and selection of wildlife. It is charming, beautiful, and most visitors fall head over heels in love with it as soon as they arrive. It is also a great place to visit for the budget traveler, as there are many free and cheap things to experience here. Here is a list of the best free and cheap things to do on Kauai Island:

- Hike the Kalalau Trail – If you are a keen hiker, Kauai is perhaps the best island for you to visit. One of the many amazing trails that are perfect for hiking is the Kalalau Trail, which follows an 11-mile stretch of the impressive Napali Coast.
- Visit Waimea Canyon in Koke'e State Park – This enormous canyon that stretches 2 miles wide and 10 miles long, with a gigantic depth of 3,500 feet, is truly is an astonishing site. It is worth checking the weather conditions, however, as it can be slightly dangerous when rainy.
- Kilauea National Wildlife Refuge – For a really small fee, check out the Kilauea National Wildlife Refuge, which is the most northern point in Hawaii and offers a really unique and memorable spot for bird and wildlife lovers. Even if you are not a particular fan of nature, there are some stunning views.
- Explore Kauai's River – One thing you will not see a lot of throughout the Hawaiian Islands are rivers. Kauai, however, has a select few rivers that are unique and enjoyable. Make sure to check them out, particularly the Hanalei River on the North Shore.

- Discover the historic towns of Kauai – In Kauai there are several old, historic towns; one of which is Koloa, which dates back to the 19th century when it was Hawaii's first sugar plantation. Another great one to visit is Hanapepe, with is in the southwest of the island. This is a great way to spend an afternoon, as you feel like you have been transported back in time.
- Take a trip to the Wailua River – Head to the scenic area that the Wailua River runs through. This place has a really sacred importance to the Hawaiian people, and it is enjoyed by many tourists every year.
- Explore the Alekoko Fishpond – Built around 1,000 years ago, the Alekoko Fishpond is a habitat for endangered Hawaiian birds, and it is said to have been built by the mythical Menehune people of Hawaii. Visitors are captivated by the unique history of the fishpond and the beautiful surrounding views.
- Relax at Lydgate Beach Park – Kauai has some stunning beaches and one of the best is Lydgate Beach Park. It is entirety free and if you have your own snorkeling gear this is a great place to experience some marine life. Alternatively, just relaxing on the sand with a good book is also a fantastic option.

- Admire the views at Hanalei Valley Overlook – One of the best places to admire the stunning views of Kauai is from the Hanalei Valley Overlook. Near to Princeville, this spot offers some of the most magical and memorable views of the colorful landscape below.
- Browse at the Hanapepe Art Night – If you are an art lover, the town of Hanapepe is a great place to visit. It is a small historic town that has a very artistic vibe. Every Friday evening, visitors can wander around and see some beautiful local artwork, as well as other forms of entertainment.

How to Eat on a Budget

Food in Hawaii is incredibly unique and has altered throughout the centuries. Between 200 and 500 A.D., the early Polynesians arrived on the Hawaiian Islands, and at this point, the cuisine was primarily meat-based and they also sourced fish from the ocean. Everything changed food-wise when in 1778, James Cook, a prominent British captain, arrived in Hawaii and brought with him a Western influence. Hawaiian food was never the same again. In addition, workers from around the world began to flock to the islands, each bringing with them their own food cultures, giving it a real mix, some of which included Portuguese, Japanese, and Chinese. In modern day Hawaii, food is a real part of the national identity, and it continues to bond people and be at the heart of the community. Here are some of the best dishes to look out for when visiting the islands:

- Lau Lau – translating as "leaf leaf," this fascinating dish consists of ti and taro leaves, often enveloping pig and fish in the center where it is then cooked over a long period of time in a rock oven. This recipe dates back to the times of the ancient Polynesians and it is still well-loved today.

- Luau – This unique Hawaiian dish is a cooked octopus wrapped in taro leaves, with coconut milk, and it has an incredibly delicious flavor and texture. It can also be made with squid or chicken.
- Purple Sweet Potatoes – Otherwise known as "uala," these unique and exciting purple sweet potatoes were first transported to the Hawaiian Islands by the early Polynesians. These potatoes are often cooked by being baked, grilled, or steamed, and can be served with a variety of other condiments.
- Breadfruit – This unique fruit is something that many people have never heard of; it was brought to Hawaii by the earliest Hawaiians between 200 and 500 A.D. and it is a large green ball-shaped fruit that has a really sweet and delicious flavor and texture.
- Kulolo – For those with a sweet tooth, make sure you check out this famous Hawaiian dessert. Kulolo consists of grated taro, and has a really thick texture and nutty flavor. Like many of Hawaii's recipes, this one also dates back to ancient times.

Where to Eat on a Budget – Big Island:

- Daniel Thiebaut – For some delicious food at a really cheap price, an option that is particularly popular with the locals is Daniel Thiebaut, which is one of the best restaurants on the whole of the Big Island. Here, you can sample some astonishing Asian-French delicacies, as well as some local music.
- Hilo Farmers Market – Hilo Farmers Market has been running almost twenty years and is held every Wednesday and Saturday in the historic center of Hilo. Here, you can experience a huge and varied selection of local foods, particularly with a focus on fruits and vegetables.
- Kona Tacos – For a really cheap price, without compromising on quality, check out Kona Tacos, which is a great restaurant in the Lanihau Shopping Center. They have some of the best tacos, tortillas and burritos on the whole island, and they have a real Hawaiian twist.
- Kaleo's Bar and Grill – For a fun and authentic Hawaiian experience for very cheap prices, make sure to check out Kaleo's Bar and Grill, which is located in a historic plantation building in the quirky town of Pahoa. There are lots of

traditional dishes, and a contemporary vibe, with lots of live music.
- Lucy's Taqueria – Situated in the heart of downtown Hilo, Lucy's Taqueria restaurant is the perfect place for those who love meat, and exotic types of meat especially. It has a very Mexican influence that is also merged with traditional Hawaiian dishes.
- Ono Seafood – Ono Seafood, as the name suggests, is the perfect eatery for seafood lovers. It is cheap, with fast service and incredible quality. Situated on Kapahulu Avenue, this eatery is central and completely irresistible. You will find yourself coming back for more!

Where to Eat on a Budget – Oahu:

- Helena's Hawaiian Food – This fantastic restaurant opened 1946 after a Chinese-American woman set up shop, serving customers incredibly delicious fusion food. Today, the restaurant is still going and is adored by tourists and locals alike.
- Waiola Shave Ice – For something a little refreshing at a very reasonable price tag, check out Waiola Shave Ice, which serves some of the brightest and most colorful shaved ice on the

whole island of Oahu. It is made on site with fresh cane sugar.

- Alicia's Market – Located in Honolulu right by the airport, Alicia's Market is the best location to visit for food if you are someone who adores fresh ingredients and the hustle and bustle of the market. There is a huge range of dishes that are often very affordable. It is also a great place to visit on a day out.
- Rainbow Drive-In – Right near the famous Waikiki Beach, the popular Rainbow Drive-In serves some of the best food on the whole island, some of the menu items include barbecue beef, burgers, and fried eggs. It is totally iconic, and a hit with locals and tourists equally.

Where to Eat on a Budget – Maui:

- Leoda's Kitchen and Pie Shop – If you have a sweet tooth, make sure to check out Leoda's Kitchen and Pie Shop in Lahaina, in Maui. Here, you can find some sweet treats, including pies, crackers, and caramels, all without breaking the bank.
- Star Noodle – One of the most popular places to eat on island of Maui, Star Noodle is always incredibly busy, so make sure you time it right. Here, you can find Asian-fusion dishes, with a

focus on noodles that are incredibly reasonably priced, and so delicious.

- Ululani – If love the famous Hawaiian shaved ice, make sure to check out Ululani, which is a shaved ice chain. Here, you can find colorful and delicious treats that are suitable for those on a shoestring budget.
- Tin Roof – In the heart of Kahului is the famous Tin Roof restaurant. Here, for less than $10, you can have one of the most delicious dishes on the entire island. The restaurant has won several awards and has a really local and authentic feel to it.
- Tasty Crust – Located in Wailuku, discover the famous Tasty Crust eatery, where you can find cheap, simple, and delicious dishes that are influenced by Polynesian classics. This is a great way to sample local cuisine on a budget.

Where to Eat on a Budget – Lanai:

- Coffee Works – For a refreshing ice coffee, make sure to check out Coffee Works in Lanai City, which serves some of the best drinks on the entire island, for very cheap.
- Blue Ginger Café – Situated in the heart of Lanai City is a beautiful café called Blue Ginger cafe, which is an ideal location for a light, delicious,

and healthy lunch. It has high-quality food and service for a very reasonable price.

- Café 565 – Another great option for budget travelers to Lanai is Café 565, which often has very long queues, but it is well worth the wait for some of the best dishes in the city of Lanai. It is very cheap and is popular with locals and tourists alike.

- Anuenue Juice Truck – Anuenue Juice Truck is a great place to visit for a spot of lunch in the sunshine, particularly if you are vegan, vegetarian, or just into healthy eating. It is reasonably priced for the quality, and it has a wonderful atmosphere.

- Richard's Market – if you love sampling local ingredients and cooking at home instead of always eating out, make sure to check out Richard's Market in Lanai City where you can find some great Hawaiian options.

Where to Eat on a Budget – Molokai:

- Molokai Burger – Situated in Kaunakakai in Molokai is the famous Molokai Burger joint where you can buy cheap but delicious burgers.

Each burger costs around $5 and is so tasty you will find yourself coming back for more.

- Ono Fish and Shrimp Food Truck – This fantastic food truck serves some of the most delicious food on the island of Molokai. It is incredibly cheap, but the quality and quantity are not compromised. This food truck often has very long queues because it is just so good, so be prepared to wait, it is worth it!
- Kamoi Snack-n-Go – For something a little sweeter and refreshing, make sure to check out the brilliant Kamoi Snack-n-Go, where you can find some gorgeous Hawaiian ice cream. There are lots of options and it is very reasonably priced.
- Kanemitsu Bakery – At Kanemitsu Bakery in Kaunakakai in Molokai you can find some of the most delicious and irresistible treats that will satisfy your sweet tooth. It is also very cheap and has an authentic Hawaiian feel to it.
- Maka's Corner – Uncover some delicious and authentic Hawaiian food at Maka's Corner, which serves great comfort food. Though it is not fancy, it is delicious, and a great place to eat in if you are a budget traveler.

Where to Eat on a Budget – Kauai:

- Kauai Culinary Market – There are a lot of local farmers markets on the island on Kauai, but perhaps the best of all is the Kauai Culinary Market, held every Wednesday from 15:50 – 18:00pm. Here, you can discover some really cheap but gorgeous homemade food and produce.
- Kauai Community College – This unique way of eating is a great experience for budget travelers. Head to the Kauai Community College in Lihue and be served delicious lunch on the cheap by young chefs. It is a cheap and fun way to eat whilst supporting the local community.
- Da Crack Mexican Grinds – If you are a fan of Mexican food, make sure to check out De Crack Mexican Grinds in Kauai. Here, you can discover some great, colorful dishes for a very small price tag.
- Kilauea Bakery and Pan Hana Pizza – For something a little bit sweeter, make sure to check out Kilauea Bakery, where you can find loads of delicious sweet treats. The Pan Hana Pizza is also great for savory items on the cheap.
- Opakapaka Grill and Bar – If you love food that is cheap but nonetheless well-presented and

suitable for Instagram photos, make sure to check out Opakapaka Grill and Bar, which serves colorful and healthy dishes inspired by local ingredients.

Best Money-Saving Websites to Book your Trip

One of the best ways to save money when traveling to the Hawaiian Islands is simply to know where to book your flights and accommodation, as this can save you so much money, before you even get there. Here are the top websites where you can book your flights, accommodation, as well as tours, to ensure that you save the most amount of money possible:

Flights – Flights are inevitably going to be one of the most expensive parts of your travels to the Hawaiian Islands, simply because of their isolated geographical position; however, there are ways in which you can save money. Check out these websites to direct you to the cheapest prices and deals, and also give you guidance on the cheapest dates to fly:

Kayak – Kayak is a great search engine that you can utilize to find the cheapest flights for your desired day of travel; you can also sometimes get great deals on Kayak when you book flights and a hotel through them, though it is advised to shop around a little first.

Skyscanner – Another great option for booking flights in addition to Kayak, is to use Skyscanner. Here, you will be re-directed to websites that have the absolute best prices, and if you are not fussy about which date that you fly, Skyscanner will tell you which is the best date to fly, and then you can work about that.

Momondo – Momondo is another fantastic metasearch website that serves travelers throughout thirty international markets. It will redirect you to the cheapest flights on the internet, and it is super easy to use and navigate.

Booking Directly – Occasionally, some of the airlines that fly to Hawaii offer some incredible deals and offers directly through their websites, especially if you have a rewards card with them, so it is definitely worth shopping around before committing to the first flight that you see.

Accommodation – Having somewhere comfortable to stay when traveling is a fundamental part of any trip away, particularly if you are spending long sunny days hiking around the beautiful scenery of the Hawaiian Islands. It can be difficult to know where to start, especially if you are looking for the cheapest possible accommodation, which Hawaii is well-known for not having an abundance of. Here are the best websites to book accommodation through that will save you the most money as possible:

Trivago – If you are someone who prefers a hotel and your own space over a hostel bunk or a private home, Trivago is undoubtedly the best platform to find the cheapest prices out there. It redirects you to the cheapest websites for the location and dates that you have entered, and gives you lots of flexibility.

Hostelworld – If you are seeking a hostel during your stay in the Hawaiian Islands, whether it is for the price, or simply just to meet people, Hostelworld is your best bet for finding the lowest prices. There are a huge number of listings, and it is incredibly easier to find cheap deals.

Hostelbookers – Alternatively, Hostelbookers is a brilliant website through which to book your hostel stay; the website has a keen focus on finding the best prices for your desired location, and it heavily emphasizes the social side of staying in hostels.

Airbnb – Alternatively, rent an Airbnb for your time in Hawaii, whether it be a private room, an entire apartment or house, this is a great way to really feel at home in a new place. It is also a great place to interact with the locals, stay in new and off the beaten track areas, and save a lot of money.

Book Direct – occasionally, you might find that the actual hotel or hostel website offers some of the cheapest deals when you book directly through them, so it is well worth having a shop around before committing.

Tours – Tours can be a great way to experience a new destination, as you can learn facts you did not previously know, understand the location in a different light, engage with the locals, and meet new people. These tours can often be very expensive, however.

Cheap Tours Hawaii – This brilliant website has an array of different offers for fun activities and tours to do across all of the Hawaiian Islands, ranging from helicopter tours to various land and water activities.

Airbnb Experience – A relatively new feature, the home rental website also offers a brilliant experience option, where locals in a particular destination can offer their expertise to visitors, whether it be a cooking class, a walking tour, or another type of workshop, this is a fun and engaging way to experience something new, at a very small price.

How to Keep Safe

The Hawaiian Islands are, on the whole, very safe to visit for tourists from other countries. The locals are friendly and welcoming, crime rates are generally low, and there are advanced hospitals and health care options. There are some things to look out for, however, and ways in which you can make yourself and those you are traveling with extra safe:

Personal Safety – Like anywhere in the world, personal safety is incredibly important. This means, keeping your valuables and important documents in your hotel room or safe in your hostel, ideally in secure or locked place. If this is not possible, take them with you. Likewise, when on the beach, leave any non-essential valuables at your accommodation and keep an eye on them while at the beach, especially touristy beaches, as these are ideal for pick-pocketing. Another great tip is to carry credit and travel cards, rather than cash where you can.

Mosquito Bites – Mosquitoes are always around in Hawaii due to its warm and sunny climate; though the diseases that mosquitoes carry, such as Zika and dengue, are not native to the islands, so the risk of getting them is relatively low. To be on the safe side, however, make sure you bring with you lots of mosquito repellent, leave your windows and doors shut, and wear long-sleeved and long-legged clothing where you can.

Sun Protection – As Hawaii has a tropical climate, it is so important to be safe in its blistering summer sun and heat. This means at all times wearing appropriate clothing, bringing lots of sunscreen and applying it regularly, as well as some high-quality sunglasses to protect your eyes. Other safety measures include brimmed hats and refillable water bottle so that you can stay hydrated when venturing outside.

Being Safe on Land – Because the Hawaiian Islands have so much natural scenery to uncover, it can be tempting to veer off the tourist track for a sense of adventure. But there can be many dangers in doing this, such as stepping on unsecure edges, rough areas where you may get lost, and the unpredictability of the weather conditions. To stay safe, ensure that you stay on designated paths.

Driving Safety – Like with hiking, make sure that you stay on track when driving around the Hawaiian Islands, as you could easily get into a dangerous area. Before heading out, make sure that you know the route, and check if there are any road closures. Also, make sure that your driving license is in date.

Weather Safety – The weather in Hawaii is very unpredictable and it is often subject to tropical storms, hurricanes and flooding; however, there are ways that this is monitored by the National Weather Service Central Pacific Hurricane Center in Honolulu. It is nonetheless good to be aware of the risks and dangers. Local issues will be broadcast if there are any potential dangers.

Water Safety – One of the biggest dangers in the Hawaiian Islands for tourists is swimming in waters that are too dangerous. There are many accidents every single year where swimmers venture out in to choppy waters when they have been warned against it. To ensure this does not happen, follow the guidance of each particular beach, and also use your common sense.

Coral Reefs and Jellyfish – A popular thing that many visitors do when they come to the islands is explore the coral reefs and the abundance of beautiful natural wildlife that lives under the water. These can be very dangerous, especially if you accidentally touch the wrong one, it can lead to very bad infections.

Here are the Visitor Assistance numbers for the main Hawaiian Islands:

Oahu – (808) 926-8274

Maui – (808) 244-3530

Kauai – (808) 482-0111

Big Island/Hawaii Island – Kona: (808) 756-0785 Hilo: (808) 756-1472

Top-Tips and Hacks to Save Money

Overall, the Hawaiian Islands can be a very pricey place to visit, from the long and expensive flights, the accommodation, and even just going for a bite to eat and a few drinks. It is not impossible to travel here on a strict budget, however, as there are many hacks that you can use to save huge amounts of cash. Here are some of the best ways to save money and still get the most out of your trip when visiting the Hawaiian Islands.

- Off Season - One of the best ways in which you can save money when visiting the Hawaiian Islands is by visiting during the low season; accommodation is far cheaper, the crowds are fewer, and flights are a lot more affordable.
- Avoid Booking too much – Another great way to save money is to not overbook activities before you even arrive in Hawaii. It can be tempting before you visit to have a load of fun things planned and booked, but this can really add up. Alternatively, book a select few and book the rest when you have arrived, as you will find they are often a lot cheaper.

- Eat like a Local – If you are a real foodie, and also have a strict budget, one of the best things you can do is to eat like a local when visiting the islands. This means doing some research about each area and seeking out the best local eateries. These will likely be far cheaper than the classic tourist trap restaurants, and also be far more delicious.
- Eat at home – Alternatively, a way of saving money if you are not particularly bothered about eating out and trying different foods, is to rent an apartment or stay in a hostel that has a kitchen. This way, you can buy ingredients from the supermarket and make your own meals, which will prove a lot cheaper.
- Don't be Reckless – Avoid making the mistake that many visitors make to the islands and avoid dangerous waters and venturing off of hiking trails. This can result in enormous hospital bills that could have otherwise been avoided.
- Free Activities – One of the best ways in which you can save money in Hawaii while still making the most of your time there, is to see out the free activities that are on offer. These include activities such as hiking, walking along the beach, and watching sunsets. You don't always need to

indulge in expensive recreational activities to have an amazing time!

- Be Flexible – Before you even go to Hawaii, consider being flexible with your dates of travel. Unless you really only can visit during the summer vacation period, by being flexible, you can find some incredible deals with flights and accommodation.
- Consider Booking a Package Trip – Another option that can often be a lot cheaper than booking things independently is to consider booking a package trip that consists of flights, accommodation, and car rental. This takes the weight off your shoulders and can drastically cut your costs.
- Travel in a Large Group – Often this is not possible, but if it is, this is a great and fun way to save money when travelling to the Hawaiian Islands. It can often make accommodation cheaper, as well as transport, such as car rentals, or even taxis.
- Don't Stay in the most Touristy Parts – Across all of the islands, there are more expensive and touristy parts, as well as cheaper, and more local parts. A great way to save money is to avoid the touristy areas where possible, and stay in more local regions. This is also a great way to

experience the islands, as it feels far more authentic.

- Plan your Finances in Advance – Rather than indulging in the first nice restaurant that you walk past, check things like TripAdvisor in advance so that you have some expectations of price and quality. Moreover, before you even leave to go to the islands, plan how much you want to spend overall and break it down day by day so you are organized and savvy with your spends.
- Have a Picnic on the Beach – A great way to save money without compromising on the overall experience is to be creative with your time and spends. One option is to have an afternoon picnic on the beach, as you can buy groceries in the supermarket and take them to the beach, rather than paying a premium for a beach-side restaurant, head to the beach yourself for food and drinks!
- Stick to one Island – If you are planning a budget trip to Hawaii, but you are not staying for a long period of time, one option is to just stick to one of the islands rather than traveling around all of them. Flights between them are really expensive and you could just thoroughly explore one

instead of stretching out the trip and spending more money.

- <u>Work or Volunteer</u> – If you are planning on staying in the Hawaiian Islands for a longer period of time, a great way to do this is to get a temporary job. This way, you can earn and explore at the same time, and really indulge yourself in island life. Alternatively, some charities and companies take on volunteers in exchange for food and accommodation, which is a fun and rewarding way to spend your time!